Arrival and Exile

Also by SUBHASH KAK

The Architecture of Knowledge
The Nature of Physical Reality
The Astronomical Code of the Ṛgveda
The Gods Within
Computation in Ancient India
Matter and Mind: The Vaiśeṣika Sūtra of Kaṇāda
Mind and Self: Patañjali's Yoga Sūtra and Modern Science
The Prajñā Sūtra: Aphorisms of Intuition
The Wishing Tree
In Search of the Cradle of Civilization
The Aśvamedha
The Loom of Time

Arrival and Exile
Selected Poems

Subhash Kak

Mount Meru Publishing

Library and Archives Canada Cataloguing in Publication

Kak, Subhash, 1947-
[Poems. Selections]
         Arrival and exile : selected poems / Subhash Kak.

"The poems selected for this volume are from books The Conductor of the Dead, The London Bridge, Secrets of Ishbar, The Chinar Garden, Eka Tāla Eka Darpaṇa, and Miṭṭī kā Anurāga as well as magazines such as Muse India."

Issued in print and electronic formats.
Poems in English and in Hindi.
ISBN 978-1-988207-15-5 (paperback).--ISBN 978-1-988207-16-2 (html)

I. Title.
PR9499.3.K27 A89 2016   821'.914   C2016-904817-9
                                                              C2016-904818-7

The views expressed in this book belong solely to the authors and do not necessarily reflect the views of the publisher. Neither the authors nor publisher is liable for any loss or damages resulting from the use of information presented in this book. Neither the authors nor publisher makes any representation or warranty with respect to the accuracy or completeness of the information presented in this book.

Published in 2016 by:
Mount Meru publishing
P.O. Box 30026
Cityside Postal Outlet PO
Mississauga, Ontario
Canada   L4Z 0B6
Email: mountmerupublishing@gmail.com

ISBN 978-1-988207-15-5

Front cover image: Black Swans in Swan River, Perth. Photograph by Subhash Kak.

CONTENTS

PUBLISHER'S NOTE

We are happy to publish this volume of selected poems by Subhash Kak (**सुभाष काक**). The volume is unique that it presents both his English and Hindi poems. This selection covers a long period with the oldest written in Kashmir and the most recent in Stillwater, Oklahoma.

Kak's poetry uses simplicity of form and themes as a means to speak of the deepest experience and he uses the tension between the two in ingenious ways. The eminent Hindi scholar Govind Chandra Pande compared his poetry to that of William Wordsworth.

We hope this volume will bring Kak's poetry to a wider readership around the world and encourage new translations.

The poems selected for this volume are from *The Conductor of the Dead, The London Bridge, Secrets of Ishbar, The Chinar Garden, Eka Tāla Eka Darpaṇa,* and *Miṭṭī kā Anurāga* as well as magazines.

PART I: JOURNEYS

1. THE TRAVELER

The traveler in his drafty room
late at night
is exhausted by the rain;
he has counted shadows
across the dark wall
of his room
when lightning struck
again and again.

It is getting colder
and from the changed beat
from the tin-roof
he knows that
it is beginning to snow.

He is reminded
of the celebration at home
for the first snowfall --
the family huddled around the furnace
drinking of hot soup and tea
boisterous games
under the kerosene lamp
snatches of stories heard
and the girl from the neighborhood
with bewitching eyes.

He plays a hill-song
on his flute
that lifts above
the patter of the rain
and the thump of the snow
sliding down the roof
to the married caretakers
who creep closer
to each other.

2. AT THE CROSSING

Journeying for several days
in heat and dust
across the desert,
sheets of rain
deluged us
as we reached
the great congregation
on the expanse
where two rivers meet.

I had marched alone first
and then joined a group
but in time I became
like a drop in a swollen stream
rolling along to
the vast gathering.

Light and dark
the waters met.

Beneath the outer calm
beyond the inner churning
some made the crossing
to the other side.

3. LOSS AND LOVE

The sparrow that built its nest
feeds the chicks without rest.
Why does the sparrow toil?
The chicks will fly away
one day.

An eagle swooped down
and stole the chicks.
The sparrow darts here and there,
searching in corners
picking twigs
letting out shrill screams.

What is love?
A mirror to an expansion,
it is like rain
on a mountain path
on a steamy afternoon
on a track that goes
round a bend.

Some tracks
fall off the mountain.

4. A PRAYER

It was from prayer books
that I learned to adore you with names.

Words are like bamboos
lashed together
across a mountain chasm.

When I lost my path
I needed more than words
to join my journey.

I have seen your image now.
The music of your creations
has become one with me
and I know that worship
is the happiness of walking
to the wilderness.

Words bind---
the smile on your face
has liberated me.

5. ACROSS THE TABLE

Across the table
in the crowded room
I found two big pools
of your eyes.

Behind the quiver
of your lips
and shy sideways glances
I saw many hidden selves --
creatures of the depths
in a mountain lake.

There was a longing for love
beyond mind and motherhood
a fear of fullness
dying and rebirth.

6. STORM IN BATON ROUGE

The storm has hung over us for days:
the rain looks like drops in a hall of mirrors.
The ground beneath the crepe myrtle is red
with fallen flowers and decaying leaves.

Gusts of wind catch the rain and smash it
against my window like the beat of a musical score.
The churning of the red dust in the garden
has yielded a shallow pool
where a dried branch has become a raft for ants
trying to reach the sheltered corner of the wall.

I go to the back porch to bring things inside
and find a frog in my outdoor shoe,
descendent of other frogs in previous years
who made that shoe their home.

The shivering birds in the branches
are braving it out;
my parrot follows me around the house
repeating the same tune as if asking:
When will the rain stop?

7. DESERT ROAD

Driving towards the setting sun
in the only car on the highway
through the unending cactus-fields on the mesa
I think of past journeys
over the *kumkum* fields of Pampore.

After the ritual of coin-offerings at the road shrine
the driver begins the climb to the plateau.
I feel alone in the straining, crowded bus
crossing the yellow splash of saffron,
with the hills dappled in different lights.
Soon, darkness loosens her skirt
over the rim of the mountains.

This is a short evening
the curtain fell quickly.
I shiver in the cool air
streaming through the open windows of the bus.

I do not know that the chamber
that holds the memory of this journey
will be opened by the cacti
in the desert.

8. TEA-HOUSE IN BUSAN

The tea-house stands on the rise on the hill road
elegant reminder of old tradition
it offers comfort to weary travelers.
Over tea cup,
the jasmine mingling with the blossoms on the trees,
I could see the road
snake into another valley
and on the west
the sea and the setting sun.

The place is quiet now
but for tourists posing for pictures
against the view from the deck
under the curving, ornate roof.

For tea we must walk across
to the restaurant beyond the hill
where nubile girls entertain
singing to guitars and harp.

9. MANILA PALIMPSEST

Memory's many layers on the canvas when peeled
splendour of the shamanic past,
hazy image of Panyupayana,
north Indian islands,
traders searching for gold
silver, spice and beauty.

It is distilled at the Villa Escudero plantation
two hours away
through lovely little settlements.
Here meet water and village,
tradition and quest for gold,
old and new.

Sit on a chair on the shallow river bed
or wade your way across to the edge of the waterfall
listen to your own voice in the muffled noises
of the excited picnickers.

I walked over to the museum
to see the likenesses of the old chiefs
and counted the fifty-four beads
of an old rosary.

10. MIRROR

Going up the mountain path,
guided by the cawing of the raven,
pulled by the scent of wild flowers
and forest pine,
I hear the faint gurgles of a rivulet.

This journey to nowhere brings calm
like the trek in the rolling sands of the desert
the cacti fields of the highland
the ocean-edge
seeing the setting sun
on a distant island.

Calm is loving,
seeing oneself mirrored
in another pair of eyes.

11. RAIN

It is the rainy season again
but like always
I've forgotten my umbrella at home.

I am stranded now
in the bazaar
waiting for the rain to stop
watching cars in the street
through the gaps in the sheet of water
falling beyond the awning.

Waiting,
watching each other
through a cloak of detachment,
imagining lives
from appearances,
joking,
we move closer,
planting our feet,
a wee bit closer.

Then suddenly
the sun broke through the clouds
and as the falling drops
scattered into many rainbows
we hurried to our next station.

12. SIGNS

Before an earthquake
animals turn anxious
snakes and rats
leave their holes
dogs wail.

Birds know the time
when they must fly
to their summer stations
on flights
thousands of miles long.

How do they prepare
for such journey?

We don't know
what we must do.
All we remember
is that we have lost
something.

That's why we are looking around
for signs
in strangers' eyes
in random events
seeking
friendships
longing
for new voices
to tell us
what we must do next.

Perhaps the signs are already there
around us
screaming
but we don't recognize.

13. REMEMBERING HOME

Home is not the place
where I was born
it is a corner of my mind
with its coded sounds
smells
the sharp seasons
which
appears to be lost
in the heap of memories.

Senses are dull now
airconditioning has banished
the seasons.

Separated from the rhythms
of cosmos
from voices of children
and animals
separated
is the body and soul
in pain.

14. LURKING PAST

Beneath appearances
lie nails
and dead selves.

It is not true
that only the present matters.
The past hides behind the present
in a thousand different shadows
that stretch and shrink
what lies before us.

15. FALLING STARS

Man is a rock
that is weathered
by rain, wind and snow.

Man is a falling star
burning bright
to scatter into
many stones.

Man is a flame
that feeds off itself
to rise into the sky.

He is a bolt of lightning
that illuminates
the shape of things
foretells the coming of rain.

Man is a root,
entwined with others,
that nourishes the plant
whose dried flowers
dot the rocks
in the landscape.

16. WHY I HAVEN'T REPLIED

I haven't replied
to your messages
because the line has been noisy
and I've not been sure
if it was you
or someone else.

The phone rings
and there is a hurried hello
the voice seems like yours
but I am not fully sure
and as I eagerly wait
for the next words
it becomes more crackly
and I can't catch
what you are saying.

I blurt out
where I am going
and how the weather is
pretending I had heard you
and then I just hang up
believing that you'd think
that the line went dead.

17. CHILDREN

Children are our teachers
they show us our blind spots
and we see
what irks us about them
is present
in us too.

Children show us
in their excitement
their dreams
and our concern
is that we may be unable to hide
how much life will disappoint.

Children insist
they must do
what we hoped
but were afraid to do.

They are more honest
because they see themselves
in us
and often
forgive us.

18. IN UPTOWN NEW ORLEANS

In this town of cafes
and jazz
I felt a connection
to my city of youth--
Delhi.

This link is the sense
of wilted flowers
of forgotten shapes
and colours.
It is the joining of college days
across two generations:
my father, me
and my son.

But New Orleans drowned –
trees uprooted
knocked down power poles
sealed moldy refrigerators
curbside.
As soldiers kept residents
out of the city,
we saw
a lonely,
starving dog
keep guard at the door
of his abandoned home.

In Delhi, the mayhem is different:
disguised bombers
from the enemy's secret army
shoot teachers and artists
and revelers in the street.

19. BOONE, NORTH CAROLINA

Near the highest hills
of the eastern continent
meditators in the hall
search for solace
in escape
from Leviathan.

Sun is streaming through the cool breeze
in the courtyard
of the vegetarian restaurant
on the main road
and then students arrive --
dressed up
to show support
for the local football team.

We climbed Grandfather Mountain
that evening.

20. LAFAYETTE

Research buildings
where professors
use their combinatorial intelligence
to think of new molecules
and circuits
that would make them rich.

My brother and I
walk through this cold city
trying hard to weave it
into the tapestry of the memories
we had with our father
fifty years ago
along the banks of
Kulgam's Vishav river.

The riverbed was vast
filled with boulders
and the water flowed
in middle in the deeper channel
like a silver ribbon
where the bridge was a
narrow plank.
I lost my balance
and fell in the water.

Here walking
by the dark waters of wide Wabash
I see nothing like the ancient temple
with its springs
the well-trodden train
the wayside vendor
the voices of the playing children
to calm my heart.

21. CLOUDY WINTRY DAY IN BOSTON

My window overlooks Harvard square
and on this cloudy morning
I watch the pedestrians
cross the streets
avoiding iced puddles
on the pavement
darting to the bookshop
and restaurants
alighting from buses.

I am reminded of the view
from my room
at the main bazaar
near Nagabal in Anantnag.
They had different caps
and they wore loose pherans
but the same spirit moved them
as they shopped
and assembled at the corner
to catch the morning bus
to Pahalgam.

22. HARWAN'S POND

It was the picnic at Harwan
with the carpets spread on the grass
and the women making tea
in the samovars
while the men
politely nodded.

We raced around
the sloping scarp of the pond
playing children's games
falling
rolling –
the other picnickers
surely thought
that college education
had crazed us.

There is an ache now
to be on that ground
to trace the hill.

23 WINTER'S DISCONTENT

There is not much to show
for the labour of the previous seasons.

What has seemed a triumph
in the bright light of the summer sky
has turned dull,
and insignificant.

If I had not done what I did
it wouldn't have changed the world.

I think no one noticed
the designs we drew on sand
and in the corn fields
and now it doesn't matter
since the harvest has been done.

24. CAPRI

The mountain in the sea
witness to the fires of Vesuvius
witness to the defilement
of the temples to the gods.

Now the refuge
from the cloying symmetry
of the city and the
emptiness of the farm.
Here come those
tired of the beauty
of the city's pavilions
and the falseness
of its spectacles.

There are no deceptions here.
The temples of Rome and Napoli
may have fallen
even Capri's altars razed
but the gods still reside here
in the wind that rises suddenly
and the force of water
smashing the sides of the boat
that brought us here.

We walk the lanes
of Capri and watch the boats
in the blue, blue sea
as we eat gelato
and then turn to see the revelers
dance tarantella.

Capri is not just for lovers.
It is solace to Europe
separated from its past

terrified of the future
here pagan gods beckon
pointing to
the mirror within
and on the mountain slopes
for answers.

25 MILLION SUNS AND THOUSAND MOONS

On Joyce Fisher's 1000-Moon Birthday

A million suns of the galaxy
twinkle as little stars
each night
and we don't notice

But ah for the joys
of the silvery light
of the one Moon
that makes tides rise and fall
in the sea
and in the depths of our being

Amongst us few have seen
a thousand Moons
mindfully.
It is a blessing
a mark of wisdom
deep insight.

It is like the solstice
that marks the birth
of the New Year
renewal of life
and light.

The Moon is the magician
who binds the child in us
with old shimmering memories
to our current self
in a tremulous embrace
edges melt
and things float
dreamily --

we free ourselves
of the certitudes of the day.

Thousand Moons
carry a secret
about time
and the mystery that sustains us
and keeps us from turning
into flower
from the longing
for the image
in the pools of water
at our feet.

26 FROZEN PIPES AND A CHAFF STOVE

Today's wintry day
takes me back to Anantnag
when an ice storm
knocked the power out
and the blackout lasted three days.

Behind our house
the public garden was a silver carpet
trees bent down
branches encased
the stream from the hot springs
of the temple
frolicked on down.

Water pipes froze
except one on the street
that faced the newspaper kiosk
around which black ice
lay congealed.

Wearing pants
over pyjamas
shivering in two sweaters
that Mother had knitted for me
I walked down the stairs to
get buckets of water
from the street tap.

Mother cooked food on the chaff stove
and we lay torpid
wrapped in heavy blankets
watching people
in the bazaar below the window
lost in the maze of memories
and dreams.

27 PAPER CUTS

Turn the leaves of memory
with care
lest they cause paper cuts.

Memories do not come alone —
one remembers
unkept promises
battles not fought
with full heart.

Love may be the state
where one does not have to
speak of it
and just be
but its moment
embraces vast domain
and there are
unspoken declarations
that do not come to be.

Memories are a fading print
and we do the turning
of the pages
mechanically
until the twinge
of the paper cut
and the muffled scream.

28 HERO ON A BICYCLE

He bicycles twenty miles
in the snowstorm
and the slush
to reach home.

He has faith
since the occasional truck
or bus on the mountain roads
can knock him off
but he has no self-pity
nor dreams of advancement
that will bring glory
to himself
and his forefathers.

He is growing old
and often his body aches
and the other day
he fell off the bicycle
and injured his knee
so he must walk with a limp.

He was watching for signs
but saw nothing
so he journeys on
patiently
by day
and starlight.

The glory he seeks
is not the one
the gods have in store for him.

29 PURA TIRTHA EMPUL

Moral law is upheld here
in the center of the Island
the domain of Vishnu
of atonement
by the drink of the amrita
in the purifying pool.

But freedom from past
is no path to freedom
for that one needs exile
not just from one's place
but one's own being
and skin
and be born again
and again
all at once.

Can one be of the city
and not
of land
and water
at the same time
be under waves
and outside.

One could use the slope
of the fire mountain
for a place
to reach up to the sky.

Or one could go to Tanah Lot
and build a temple on the rock
in the sea
where wading through the surf
the pilgrim invokes the Great Yogi.

PART II: ACROSS THE WATERS

1 THE ROLLING WHEEL

i.
In the deepest night, as Moon arose
Over countless stars in a million rows
The darkness sped away –
And I lay down on the grass for repose.

ii.
In the garden of thousand chinars in the vale
I viewed my life: a moment on the cosmic scale
My happiness drained –
I felt my life and works were to no avail.

iii.
Who really cares for a note that has died?
Should we not wish for things to abide
For ever and always?
I held my face in hands and cried.

iv.
Who is my maker and why did he make?
And why if he made, from knowledge's lake
He gave us little?
And he would, would his power be at stake?

v.
Is he afraid that his earthen toy
Will lose the power to enjoy
His fleeting life?
And in despair he will himself destroy?

vi.
As I looked around, I heard an old man cry:
Ah pain! I've learnt that to live one must die.
Each day is misery
The price for breathing is too high.

vii.
Let not the Earth dance to the Sun
Let the universe be once again unspun
That for ever ends
The meaningless race of our lives we run.

viii.
Let not the foolish dream continue
Let black be turned what is brilliant hue
Let eternally recede
The deceiving sky that shines so blue.

ix.
Illusion fills the mind with dread
Of the time when night will hang lifeless and dead
And morning
Leads to more darkness in Sun's stead.

x.
If good luck should us bring
To a day that has ever been shining
And would ever shine.
Shall we be able to see, hear, or sing?

xi.
Won't an everlasting day daze our minds?
And we search for happiness like the blind
Who will colors define?
Never in darkness does man glory find.

xii.
Can it be that no night, no day
Will follow when the dimming ray
Of night is gone?
Ah, where and when will then we stay?

xiii.
If the gods made us, then why so weak

That I must crumble before I can speak
Before I know
Before I can grasp all that's sad and bleak.

xiv.
As the man said this, he crumpled to the earth.
While a sheep said: Keep faith for birth
Of Art must be again.
A new being will rise from this broken earth.

xv.
The previous state of the soil will ensure
If the coming crop is rich or poor
And the basic laws
Will be the same whether you're sweet or sour.

xvi.
Fear not! With faith as friend
And with noble thoughts as faith, boldly wend
Though life's dark desert.
Then He will joyfully you with Himself blend.

xvii.
Now I saw another form that seemed made
Of motor parts, in symmetry laid.
It announced its triumph
Which looked more pitiful than can be said.

xviii.
The Robot said: Don't be fearful for we conquer
The haughty gods in whose judgment's fear
We have lived
At the cost of our joys, hopes, and more dear.

xix.
Follow me! I'll show you how to conquer God.
Then in victory, we will tread the road
To countless worlds.
No man will serve, for he will be the Lord.

xx.
The universe will play at our will
And with science we'll foolishness still
Even create new man
From nothingness for sweet thoughts to fill.

xxi.
Walking away from this, I thought of fate
And its twin: idea of heavenly state.
For if he makes us kill
Why should he, at judgment, be irate?

xxii.
It seems that life is like the peal of a bell
That starts in nothing and later shall
End in nothingness.
Can we free ourselves from the striker's spell?

xxiii.
Can the bell know if it ever rung before?
And why should it not, in time, ring more?
Is this the mystery
Life holds. No other wisdom in store?

xxiv.
All that's born must one day die
One will be a lifeless log though *Why*

One may cry.
The thing will happen no matter what we try.

xxv.
What's my story? I lived and died.
And who about deepest pain can write?
Why shed tears
When unknown in world I can abide.

xxvi.
Do you think my grief will Sun or Earth shake
They have seen more misery. They'd hardly quake.
When we're no more
Like always they'd sleep and wake.

xxvii.
I hope the world doesn't my memories envy
Let them sleep where they lie
And you, O Lovely One,
When you pass this chinar, just sigh.

xxviii.
I'll smile that my absence some will feel
In my hear it may some wounds heal
And the future
I'll ready to face with more steel.

xxix.
I know, as I sleep, the brilliant morn
Would again rise; the Moon will be born.
And the rolling wheel
Like always, for its goal, will roll on.

2. AWAKENING

When the first light
Opened my eyes to pulsating life
I felt around
And felt the force of form.
Curled up and protected
I looked out
And aped: so learnt.

I wove strange patterns for creation
Ruled by mysterious forces.
But of the symbols of my world
None acted as I expected
Until I knew their secret.
Amongst the living too
I saw an order
Governed by a vision,
Secret password to sensibility.

The word can't be disobeyed
Smallest breach leads to a slippery path
To contradiction.

This grief can be avoided
If the word too
Is dispensed with in a cosmic sacrifice.

3. DONKEYS

The window of my room
Opens on a quarry
Where the laborers load donkeys.

The donkeys do their part
Quietly... calmly
Walking in line ahead of the driver
Never straying from the shortest path
Like machines
Their dreamy eyes seem fixed
On some splendid vision in their minds.

No sound escapes their throats
They prod on at an even pace
While the driver stops
Grimaces with pain
Or beams at some private joy
Jumping up and down with monkeyish gestures
He catches up with the train
That quietly stops at the destination
For its load to be taken off.

I have seen this countless times
Can even tell the donkeys apart
Yet I can't help taking leave from work
To have another look at the scene:
Their nature is so mysterious
Beyond understanding.

I wonder how they get into their trance-like states
How manage to remain uninvolved.
Never needing to communicate.

I wish I knew their tongue
I would question them
To know their secret to tranquility.

But I may fail to wake them from their trance
Or perhaps they are mute.

4. FEAR

In the heat of the battle
There is no moment to grieve
For fallen friends and foes.

As one advances
Breaking memories right and left
One is scattered
Into infinitesimal fragments ...
Into nothingness.

Helpless by circumstance
Like tree bound to earth
As it is sawn and cut.
How can it feel anything?

Fear arises only when
You can change things.

5. DEATH

My friend is critically ill.

I return home from the hospital in the
Evening and go to bed.

But sleep I cannot.
As I lie tossing, a vision rises before me.

My friend is dead.

I see myself choked with sorrow,
Tears streaming from my eyes,
Consoling my friend's wife.

But what can consolation do to a departure,
A death?

I am dazed, stupefied,
Staring vacantly at the funeral
Thinking of the futility of it all
Of the lack of redemption.
Slowly I sink into a sea of forgetfulness.

Next morning, I rush to the hospital.

The waiting room is full of acquaintances
With sorrowful looks and wet eyes.
My friend's wife is sobbing in a corner.

My friend had just died, I know.
But my mind is vacant,
My face blank,
And I am speechless.

My acquaintances stare at me
Wondering at my ill manners
My lack of grief.

But what do they know? Yes, what do they?
Have I not grieved – I know how sorely –
When for me he died last night.

47

6. EXILE

Memories get hazy
even recounting doesn't help
I need to look at pictures
or listen to music to remember
and sometimes walking through narrow lanes of my
    town
a sudden perfume escaping from a window
halts my steps and I am transported
to my childhood years.
What other memories live behind the barred doors?

I hear the girl next door calling out;
I do not answer because her stern father
is watching from the balcony.
Many scents mingle in the courtyard,
the autumn breeze touches lightly on my skin.
Women are pounding grain in the giant mortar,
our hen is guarding her brood
from the mean street mongrel.

And now we glide through a water passage
over pink lilies, reeds, and rushes
against the curtain of sleek houseboats
moored to banks with soft green grass
with willow trees guarding the edge of water
and giant chinars shading higher ground.
Blue kingfishers flash across water
and yellow orioles dart from tree to tree
and now we pass a quince orchard
with blossoms of delicate pink
and a field of brilliant yellow mustard.

We stop at a clearing
where a girl is selling honey
and as we talk the sounds of cows and calves
sheep and lambs

geese and gosling
ducks and duckling
chicken and chicks
children singing tables from a canalside school
men coughing on their hookahs
float by.

The best paradise
is the paradise we are exiled from.

7. REACHING SRINAGAR

As the dusty bus crosses the Banihal tunnel
the air becomes scented and zippy
and the passengers break out into a loud cheer.

We strain into the distance
to guess where Verinag might be
to begin tracing Vitasta's course.

At Kazigund we order egg paranthas
and now the driver races through---
Kashmiri songs blaring on the radio---
Khanabal, Bijbehara
the ruins of Avantipura
the saffron fields of Pampore
and then to the kulcha shops further on.
It is quite dark when we reach Srinagar.

We wait in a corner as father gets our holdalls and trunks
and we climb aboard the tonga---
horseshoes flashing in the dark
against the asphalt of the road.

8. UP THE SINDH RIVER IN A DOONGA

It was dark when the doonga arrived at the Apple River
food, stoves, rugs, and blankets were loaded in
the beds were made in the dim lights of kerosene lamps
and soon we lay down to the sounds of the poles against
    the sides
that pushed the boat
past the shadows of other boats,
watercress and asparagus.

While we listened to stories of the cousins
and some singing of the girls
father called out the stages that were crossed:
passing under the city's bridges we reached Shadipur
and then pushed against the current of Sindh.

The boatmen were up before us next morning.
Ropes were anchored to the boat
and towed from the bank to make the climb easier.

By evening we were at Ganderbal.
Rented tongas took us to the magic spring of Tulamula.
We set up camp under a chinar tree
and played under the lights to the singing of the
    worshipers.
We peered into the water to check its colour
to know the future
but layers of flowers prevented this
so we did puja, ate luchis and nadroo fries and rested.

It was a pleasant night.
Voices around us and singing in the distance
made us feel secure. We were oblivious
of the trials that lay before us.

9. SNOW IN SRINAGAR

The radio says it has snowed in Srinagar.
The first snow is cause for celebration:
mother lit the wooden stove in the kitchen
and unwrapped packets of beans and dried vegetables
    and fish
to make the feast. And we hurried into the backyard
dragging our wooden slippers through the snow
throwing snowballs until it was time to take
packed boxes of steaming food and gifts
to the neighbours and relatives to spread merrymaking;
and we received similar things in exchange.

After our fights were over we watched
from the window the boatwomen hurrying
across the embankment to the kulcha shop
and heard the labourers pushing the overloaded carts
to mutual exhortations
across the slush of the broken pavement.
Down a flight of steps
the samovar was ever ready
with hot moghal chai and sweet kulchas.

In the evening in the big room,
wrapped in blankets over our pherans,
new kangris with painted wickerwork were started,
and as we waited for father to return from work
we listened to grandfather's tales
and the conversation between the ladies
in the kitchen.

The dinner done by the faint light of the electric bulb
we heard the day's accounting
as the thalis were cleaned with sawdust and ash.
When my feet were cold

my father took them under his blanket
and warmed them with the warmth of his own feet.

Who knew then that decades later a terror will come to
    Srinagar
and I won't see my home where I was born
where we had played cowries on many new snows.
The terrorists want to bury our past
forget the deeds of our ancestors.

We are banished because we remember
tales that grandfathers told us
because we remember
our story.

10. JOURNEY INTO THE HIMALAYAS

Remember the embers
that seemed to come back to life
from time to time
the wind springing up like a ghost violated
the tent beating its elephant flaps
forgotten maps
the waters' easy laughter
you and me
our intimacy.

Must the tramp stamp his way
through the pines
incarnations of our long-lost brothers
they have waited so long
that their memory sleeps.
When they awake
we shall be deep in slumber
remember.

Morning wakes up so languorous
the smouldering fire in flesh
the chant of birds
grass blue with dew
eyelids flutter and a smile
floats across the raw air
let the tin-warming begin
and then the brushing of hair.
Does a mountain talk?
Up the paths on the curves
in the clearings the tumescent earth
and big broken teeth of rock
lie here and there
and beyond the grass and the lichen
of the lower slopes
one can see the meditating face

of the mountain-- eyes closed
noble forehead firm nose
and during rains one can hear
the fremitus in its chest.

Have you bared your body
to some mountain stream
kissed its froth
let it rub your back
and stood free with your friend
in your large bathing field--
how haltingly does warmth return?
And when it has spread
and we are but names again
it is time to tread
the ribbon on the hill.

After the descent of clouds
the rain comes crashing down.
The ponies are shivering wet
their big sad eyes turned inwards
and a brown field mouse is smelling its way
back to its flooded hole.
Will it miss its tribe
and go searching to the river bank?

Seasons work a magic, the roots
clutch and drag at the slipping earth
and join the pine cones and sheep droppings
and scorpions being flushed down the slope.

Why must water fashion and destroy
give strength to lemmings on their last march
the wind dry and freeze
the sun warm and burn
the earth support and inter
why must entropy ever increase.
And yet new forms scream their beginnings
in the muddy bloody spring.

Who will their dirges sing
who will dig their homes in the slush of snow
or make them fires in the clearings in the woods?

That light on the hillside is no star
the shepherd must be talking to his wife
exchanging memories through words and otherwise
for each wears the smells of a hundred days
butter sweat urine other fluids
damp of the earth
curries herbs and smoke
for why should he revoke
and the camp ever so gently breathes.
Do you hear the whine of the darkness
and beard sprouting through the skin?

As the night softly smooths its sheets
no bears around no fearful sound
the body lying peacefully on the ground
why does the mind insist on a second journey
along the path well-trod by our tired limbs.

Fire and air
water and earth
are aplenty on the Himalayas.
Yet the mind rushes over early ghosts
school and father
friends and mother
car and clothes
and makes its way to the mountain hospice.
It is indeed unnecessary:
we are who we are
we are who we are
we remember.

11. ISHBAR EVENINGS

Evening brings you to the magic circle of its sound:
the chirping of chicks, hens clucking,
the little stream jumping down the rocks,
the alarm in the koel's call,
the muffled footsteps of young girls
the clang of my grandmother's wooden sandals
as she shuffles up the incline,
the ringing bells from the altar,
the repetition of holy names,
and the deep call of the boatman
that echoes from the hilltops.
Sweet, warm smells from the bakery waft up
and we are served sugared green tea
with cinnamon, cardamom and almonds
sitting on rugs in the verandah facing the altar.

The lake begins to prepare for repose
as the last shikaras slide on the surface
punctuated by the dull sounds of the oars.

On rainy evenings the water sloshes down
along new channels from down the hill's slope
and spouts out of a thousand little crevices on the surface
bringing the boil from the secret chambers of the
mountain.
And I wobble on my wooden sandals
over deep mud
to get the corn for our chickens
shivering as the cold wind gathers
under my loose shirt.

In the sacred spring the fishes
prance unperturbed,
and the crows linger forlornly
on the ancient stones.

Birds, fishes, animals on the slope
have no regrets
they fear only for their survival,
we are burdened by what we remember.

12. MY FATHER IN HAWAII

The gardens in Kaimuki recall childhood dreams:
water, sand
black crater of diamond head
like the mountain over the Dal Lake
and the little stream behind the apartment
seems like the shrunken Apple River
the fence preventing the exploration
of the lock in its way
before it meets the big water.

The park atop St. Louise Heights
with its pine trees
cool breeze
and the bowl of Manoa at our feet
like the clumps of trees
beyond the clearing of Gopadri hill.

Walking up and down the hillside above our home
was like a little pilgrimage
to the goddess of the isles
a sister to the sparrow goddess
of our old city.

We searched for him
on Haleakala
asked goddess Pele
who breathes fire and lava
drove over the winding mountains of Maui
searched again in the beaches at Lanikai
amongst the surfers at Waikiki
at the reefs of Hanauma bay
on the warrior boat
pulled by synchronized oars
returning past sunset.
The children are dazed

grasping hands
and a wail---
deeper than sorrow or regret---
emerged from the hollow of my heart.

My mother cried for months and said:
A light joined another light
in Hawaii.

13. RECORDS OF OUR LIVES

What do we do with our memories, do we
trust them completely, or do we make recordings
of each moment we live, and keep a diary
for all thoughts? Then we can audit
each recall, and if we should forget
we can go back to the books
and relive our days moment by moment
refresh any period of choosing.

But what if someone should steal my memories
and take my past for his own? Will the thief
become my twin or can I sue him
for faking his past? But what if he believes
his new past completely?

And how can I be certain that my impressions
are accurate and not transposed with some other's?
How shall we find the truth or does it matter
whose records are these anyway?

On the other hand, if we trust our recollections
and accept that we do suppress moments of youthful
     indiscretions
how do we know that what the others say about us
is false? Maybe, we broke the law several times.

So is it best to own up and confess?
Can memories return prompted by the dreams
of others or be dredged up by clever psychologists?
Are we responsible for our remembrances?
Should they be all nice and clean?
Can we borrow or buy good ones?

And if our remembrance doesn't matter,
how do we define

ourselves? How is our responsibility
measured? If memories are shaped
by those around,
where is freedom?

62

14. THREADS

When feelings are reasoned
the pain of no-feeling
soaks you
the pain
of no-feeling mocks you
and your organs burn
your cells melt
in that acid.
Ah must one burn
in one's own fire?

A question is best answered
by another question.

I have had the same dreams
for ten years
same images have haunted me
same fears oppressed.

Yogin sits at the balcony
trying to tell the passersby
she is lonely
through telepathy.
Did I hear her right?
I must examine the dregs of her tea
see her picture in a mirror
measure her shadow
read my mantra a million times
over her hair
yes she is full of desire
but soon she will tire.

A silent shriek shakes me up
I see the wraith of the village pig
I rush to the slaughter field

where the pig lies feet bound mouth muzzled
his screams rend the air
the four ape-men in loin-cloth do not hear
they are sharpening their knives
to make meat for their wives.

I fast this evening
but instead of communion with the pig's soul
I let my thoughts roam
till they stop by Anand's daughter
sixteen year old worshiper at my temple.
She is onyx to my touch
so I tell her of mysteries
of being and emptiness.

I have so much of desire
that desire itself is my fulfillment.

15. ASK KRISHNA

Why must one choose between
heaven and earth
balance yin and yang
and knowing maya yet desire
why can't one be both
here and there
please this and that
and if that cannot be
why not be neither here
nor there?
Trishanku did it.

We are alive in spite of ourselves
we have seen torsos breathing
for legs arms eyes ears
smell speech
do not make a man.
We just exist
we cannot perceive ourselves.
Let us not try lifting mounts
on little fingers.
It is futile
speaking of our nature
ask Godel.

Death swallows the earth
death swallows the hearth
the earth buries the dead
the dead haunt the earth
the earth gives birth
like serpents in one circle
cycles are endless.
Ask Krishna Buddha Abhinav Gandhi
or ask the beggar in the street
or ask me.

16. THE CONDUCTOR OF THE DEAD

i.
I am not what I look
I am my ghost.

When I was dead
my soul was rejected
in heaven and hell
and finally driven
to the refuge of my bones.

ii.
We are beautiful for we die
Once time had halted its flight
one moment was a thousand years
I was dust, O I was an idea
how I longed to be again in flesh
for I haven't felt enough
not enough
and when my frozen body thawed
with the stirrings of life
it was ecstasy.

iii.
And speech was born of silence.
Freedom may be a prison
yet stillness does not revel
in stillness
does not revel
in the throbbings of a heart
but who wants beauty
so let me sing a song
let me roll a stone
let me chime a bell.

iv.
I drink defeat everyday like my breakfast milk.
This morning when I awoke
blots of white sunlight dotted my room.
I scattered my night clothes all around my bed
yet the plates on the table
were neatly arranged
the furniture in the room
was all in its proper places
I could not eat my breakfast.

v.
The birds fled when I came
I had no knife
and I offered seed with my hands
the birds still kept away
and my arms got tired and I let go.
The scattered grain sprouted plants
with little white flowers---
what a harvest of lilies.

vi.
The last phoenix
sailed serenely to the fire
to burn
to turn into ashes
and rise again
youthful and chaste.

As it neared the fire and closed
its eyes for the plunge
it felt itself rudely swept
away--its throat firmly squeezed
that sure was no rebirth--
someone had cut its wings.

The phoenix still lies
at the same place

unmoving, unfeeling
not alive, nor dead
its life is in its eyes
that slowly move
and scan the skies.

The fire nearby
is long extinguished.

vii.
I sat on the railing
warming my bones in the winter sun.
On my eyelashes the sunbeams broke
into a million gossamer globes
and soon ants were crawling all over the place.

They came floating in
like the fragrance of death
and ate through my desires.

17. A WOUNDED BIRD

i
You said I was a bird with a broken
wing. I am afraid that when you have
nursed me to health I might fly away.

ii.
The sadness in your eyes haunts me.
When you have given me life and
I take my lonely flight (Can I help
that?) will it not break your heart?
Why do you breathe life into me, when it
will be the death of both of us?

iii.
Do not grieve at my stony face. My
heart warms to your every smile, every
touch. I almost feel the strength to
fly. Shall I get well and lose you?

iv.
That I love you is clear
since I ask you for nothing.
I would love you even if you went away
leaving my wing bleeding.

v.
I feel guilty that my condition
made you interrupt your play.
No, you have hung around me for many
days now, stroking my feathers, dressing
my wounds. Can I ever repay you?

vi.
You have whispered in my ears
that I look so weak and wan that

you must help me. And what patience!
I haven't spoken, you still console
me with your beautiful words.

vii.
Don't you realize that you are
wasting your youth on a
bird with shrivelled limbs
when your garden is full of handsome
admirers? They know many clever
games to amuse you.

viii.
I admit I have called you sometimes
with my cries.

ix.
In your absence your image has
lain with me. The shadow of
your soft hand has warmed my
feathers in the cold nights.

x.
Shall I get well and live with
you in a gilded cage woven
by your deft fingers
or shall I paint your form
on these rocks before I fly off?

18. THE RIDDLE OF ISHA

All that moves has a secret:
the spirit envelops the bones
and when you yield
you win without greed.

Regrets of a hundred years
weigh us down
unless we know the dance.

We are led to darkness
if we don't recognize the image
we saw as children.

That which never stirs
is very swift
we can't chase it down with thoughts
it will stop when one stands still.

It moves and moves not
its eye surrounds
reflects
overpowers with its magic.

This is a strange walk
to the darkness of the vault
and when we soar
the darkness beyond
the horizon in the west
is more intense.
If one could journey
to the secret of the smile
pleasures will come
without the seed of sorrow
detachment will fall
without emptiness.

Can we jump
beyond the golden disk
remember the deeds
there is
no other.

19. THE HIDDEN PATH UP THE HILL

Autumn leaves and broken branches cover this path
and it breaks off at several places
winding around huge rocks
and over little streams
where one must jump over mossy boulders.

At the end of the climb
is a bowl-like depression
with the softest grass---
sheltered by a huge canopy of branches
extending beyond the rock edge.

I have spent many afternoons at this cove
breathing its jasmine air
listening to the pigeons
and the gurgle of the rivulet.

The explorers have heard of this hollow,
they are looking for diamonds
they will blast their way up.

They will never find it.

20. A BOY AND HIS DOG

The boy hunted with his faithful dog.
They sought spaces beyond the jungle
stamped new trails
swam in forest ponds
chased birds across flowering pastures
winked at death.

Why should I be afraid, the boy asked.
Alive, we think about the time
when we are no more
when the roses have been replaced by silk
when the earth has lost its fragrance
when the shadow has fallen.
We are the walking dead.

He played with guns
and he died of a gunshot.
At the funeral his mother consoled
the mourners on their own losses.

The dog searched for the boy everywhere
and with each new day he became weaker.
His life ebbed out
with the eleventh moon.
The mother took the body at night
to the cemetery
and buried it
next to the boy.

PART III: THE SACRED VALLEY

1. MYSTICAL PYRAMID

The Sacred Valley
is the Milky Way
it is the highway of the gods
between the darkness of mountains
the Vilcanota River snakes
through its pastures and fields
its constellations are hung
on terraces
up the mountain walls.

The mystical pyramid
of nine terraces
lies hidden behind the mountain
its doorway lit up
by the winter sun
when the gods descend
to earthly domain
in processional.

The pyramid doorway
is just one of many
that connects the three worlds
there are others scattered around
in the valley
in the huacas
that the pilgrim comes to see.

As memorial of his visit
the pilgrim makes images
of the gods
at the salt flats of Maras —
this celebrates his good fortune
his small part
in the cosmic play.

2. MOUNTAIN CIRCLES OF MACHU PICCHU

Coming down the Inca Trail
the clearing of Machu Picchu
on the inner rim
opens like a lizard in repose
with a puma on the side
and then the two merge
becoming a condor
in flight
to take the measure of
the two mountain circles
around the Putucusi axis.

In caves and temples
and the huacas
there are hidden shapes
as fleeting shadows
the cosmic tree and corn
face of Tunupa
signs for the faithful.

The ancient pilgrim came
to the old mountains
before he became so wearied
that he could not walk
the steep inclines
of the Inca Trail
to see the house of gods
and arcs of light
bridging mountain tops
to see Viracocha
and hear him
in the waterfall and the
call of birds.

The modern tourist
watches the llamas
grazing on the pastures
looks at broken temples
the ruined buildings
of the observatory
finds satisfaction
in seeing the mountain fastness
and smiles at having explored the source
of the coca leaf.

3. KORIKANCHA

The abode of Inti
nourishes llamas and herders
in the plaza of Huacaypata.

Inti and Mama Killa
gave bounties to Pachamama
and the lands prospered
but the people and kings
got lost in dream time.

The temples were smashed
and the head of the Puma
at Sacsayhuaman
became a battlefield.

Cities were burnt down
rope bridges on the Inca Road
were destroyed.

The prisoner Sapa Inca cried out
"Pachamama,
see how my enemies shed my blood."

The waking up from the dream sleep
has taken years
it has been a long season of blues
the huacas were defiled
the condor flew alone in the sky.

Tupac Amaru was quartered in Huacaypata
but he did not die in vain
his fight was for liberty
and new heroes have taken his cry
across continents of the globe.

The sun is shining
in the backdoor
in its warmth old seeds
in the ground
are sprouting new plants
the flying lizard speaks to the condor
and the puma is not hungry.

4. PRAYER TO VIRACOCHA

Viracocha, do not respond to
my entreaties
my prayers have become mechanical
I am only moving my lips
my heart is stone.

My pilgrimage was a false one
I didn't think of you
as I walked the temple steps.

Let my pain get sharper
let my desire to see you
become sincere
so that what I seek
is not merely what I hear
repeated
without knowing what the words mean.

You are everywhere
you make the sun and the moon rise
make seasons
you hide in the play of light
in the shadow of the mountainside
in the craggy corners of the rocks
in waterfalls.

You know what is at the bottom of my heart
buried under the commands and instructions
of daily labors.

I am too exhausted
to remember what I knew so clearly
when I was young
and strong of body.

If you hear me now
and you grant
what is in the words I have spoken
without knowing what they mean
what would I live for then?

PART IV: मिट्टी का अनुराग

1. अंगारों का रास्ता

वीथि पर
अंगारे बिखरे हैं।
समय थोड़ा है
तलवों के छालों की
पीड़ा से परे हम
भ्रांति की ओर
बढ़ गए।

हम जानते हैं
आकांक्षा है जीवन विधान।
ज्ञानी चुप हैं
और देवता सो रहे
आराधित होने के संतोष में।

दर्शन और मीमांसा
कुछ स्पष्ट नहीं करते

केवल भाव हैं हमारे पास
तो हम क्यों न
ओंठ से ओंठ मिलाएँ।

मृत्यु हर दिन होती है
तो महाप्रयाण का
क्या भय?

2. अनुराग और द्वेष

मैं तुमसे अब प्रेम नहीं करता
यह सच है,
भले ही मुझे तुम्हारी याद
आती है।

मुझे तुमसे द्वेष है अब,
यद्यपि यह द्वेष
प्रेम का चिह्न है।

जो मैं तुम्हें
चाहता नहीं,
तुम भी मुझे
भूल गईं।

मुझे तुमसे प्रेम था,
और कदाचित
तुम्हें भी कभी
मुझसे प्रेम था।

पर तुमने मेरा नाम
अपने हृदय से
मिटा दिया,
मैं भी दूर देश
तुम्हारा अपवाद
करता हूँ।

परंतु यदि तुम्हारी दृष्टि
वाटिका के दूर कोने में
उस पेड़ पर पहुँचकर
जो मैंने बोया था
स्मृति को जगाए
और तुम मेरा नाम लो
मैं तत्काल चला आऊँगा।

3. अश्वताल

चिदम्बरम का तेज
गर्मी की भाप से
धुँधला गया है।
राख में लिपटे
चूल्हे के अंगारों में
कम जान है।
खिड़की के बाहर
नाले की पुलिया की
नींव टूटी लगती है।
और उसका रास्ता
किस गांव जाता है
अब मुझे ज्ञात नहीं।
नहीं मुझे याद है
कैसे मैं आया
इस महालय में।
वेदना आशा देती है।
संदेश है
आश्विनों के एक
प्राचीन क्रम का।
अश्वताल में शरीर
भिषज को सौंपे
मैं दर्पण में ज्योति को
टिकटिका देख रहा हूँ।

4. इतिहास पुराण

इतिहास पुराण के भीतर
छिपा है
पुराण इतिहास में।

पुराण वेदना का नामरूप
भीतर का संघर्ष-
जो कर्म नहीं हो पाए
उन पर टीका है
क्योंकि देवता आलसी हैं।

राक्षसों के पास
वासना है,
प्रेम नहीं
मित्रता नहीं
महत्वाकांक्षा है,
धार्मिक उन्माद है।
वह उपनिवेश
और साम्राज्य
माँगते हैं।

देवता श्रम नहीं करते,
संस्कृति का निर्माण नहीं करते।

अन्याय और अत्याचार
का झंझावात
चेतना को
झकझोरता है।
काली आँधियाँ चलती हैं।
संस्कृति उस को
बाँधने का जाल
नीलकंठ की तरह
विष पी लेने का
न्याय।

इतिहास को
पुराण के परिवेश में देखिए।

5. एक और युद्ध

क्योंकि वह रक्षा न कर सका
युद्ध में पराजय हुआ
प्रेमिका के हृदय में
वह अब अपमान पात्र है।
जो पुरानी स्मृतियाँ थीं उनकी
पेड़ के नीचे बातें
उद्यान में टहलना
पर्वत के छोटे पथ पर
घोड़ों पर भ्रमण
अब वह झूठ हैं।
वह झूठ था।
प्रेमी को
धिक्कार रही है वह।
क्या चाहती है,
एक और युद्ध?

6. पत्ते और भाव

पेड़ के शब्द पत्ते
और मुस्कान
फूल हैं।

शब्दों से अन्य पेड़
बँधते हैं,
पक्षी और तितलियाँ
सुनती हैं इन्हें।

हमारे भाव
पत्ते हैं
प्रफुल्लित हो जाते हैं कभी।

सिकुड़ते और मुझाते भी हैं
चिनार के लाल
पत्तों की तरह।

धरती पर गिरकर
समेटे जाते,
सुलगाकर उनके अंगारों से
गर्मी मिलती है
अंजान लोगों को
ठिठुरती सरदी में।

7. प्रेम का संकेत

मेरा तुम्हारे लिए अनुराग
एक वस्तु की इच्छा नहीं
एक छाया को देखने की अभिलाषा है
जो शरीर और आत्मा
के बीच है।

रहस्य का उद्घाटन है यह
क्योंकि इसके अंत में
न मैं मैं हूँ
न तुम तुम हो।

जहाँ पहुँचकर यदि तुम द्वार
खटकाओ
मैं न सुन पाऊँगा।

8. पशु विदाई

पशु की एक दृष्टि
कितना कह सकती है?

जिसके साथी
बीच-बीच में
लुप्त हो जाते हैं
वह क्या सोचता है
जगत का विधान क्या है?

बहुत क्रंदन होता है
बलि के पूर्व
जीवन दान की याचना
विधिवत है।
उस रोने को
हम भूल जाते हैं।
वह भूलना भी
विधिवत है।

पिपासे, व्याकुल प्राणी,
उर्वर समय की प्रतीक्षा
नहीं कर सकते।

इस काल संघात से
इंद्रियाँ जब
दुर्बल होती हैं

तब पशु से विदाई
सह्य हो जाती है।

9. रंग अँधेरे में

क्या वसंत का
नृत्य इतना सुंदर है,
कि तुम इसके रंग
रात में भी
बता सकती हो?

क्या तुम
मिट्टी की गंध
वापस बुला सकते हो?

जंगल में पेड़ों की भास
इतनी मादक है
मुझे भय है
मैं अगला श्वास भूल न जाऊँ।

वसंत के रंग
पहाड़ियों के मध्य
घाटी में फैल गए।
आकाश की तनी हुई चादर की थरथराहट
से मेरा शरीर काँप उठा

हृदय जिसने
प्रेम किया है
भूल नहीं सकता।

10. श्वेत फूल

बचपन के आँगन के
श्वेत फूल
मैं भूल गया,
जब से गाँव छोड़ा
वैसे पौधे नहीं देखे।

प्रातः कल
अमेरिका की एक नई बस्ती में
जहाँ मैं खो गया था
गाड़ी की खिड़की से
मैंने वैसे ही
श्वेत फूल
एक घर के पास पाए।

एक लड़का उस उद्यान में
खेल रहा था।
जैसे स्वप्न में
डूबा हो।

11. ग्रहण

ग्रहण के छादन में
पक्षी शाखाओं में छिप गए।
मानव चाय के प्याले पीते
चहचहाते रहे
संस्कृति सिखाती है कि
भयानक की चर्चा न हो।

जिस के लिए शब्द न हों उस की स्थिति नहीं।

अबोध बालक ने रिक्त सूर्य को घूरा।
प्रौढ़ काच लेकर उसका प्रतिमान
काग़ज़ पर देखने लगे।
हमने उस में जादू पाया
भय और अंधी आशा।

याद आया
शुक्र का सूर्य में तिरोधन
और उसके पार गमन।

12. चन्द्रमा

चन्द्रमा को केवल देखिए नहीं
नीचे ले आइए।

इसकी आकृति
अपने साथ रखिए
थैली में,
गोल पैसे की तरह।

इसे काटिए
बाँटिए।

इसे दो बनाकर
आँखों पे रखिए
सुख चैन के लिए।

13. जंगल में आग

जंगल के बीच
लहराते वृक्षों को देख
आभास हुआ
हम ही
वह बहती समीर थे।

हम चुप रहे
जब घुडसवार वहाँ पहुँचे
आग लगाने,
एक बस्ती बसाने।

हृदय स्तब्ध था,
क्योंकि हृदय रहस्यपात्र है
इस की भाषा नहीं।
और अरण्य ग्राम के सामने
हटता है।

पक्षी और पतंगें
आग के तूफ़ान में
वृक्षों के ताण्डवीय नृत्य
में झूल रहे थे,
आहुति बनकर।

14. नगर

नगर एक कारागार है।
जो धरती पर राज करे
पहले एक माली बने।

मुझे अब याद नहीं
कि मैंने यह पौधे बोए।

पुस्तक जेब में एक उद्यान है।
प्रकृति में प्रत्येक वस्तु
एक जाल में बँधी है।

फूल भी अतिथि से
मिलने को आतुर हैं।

15. नयनों का कोना

कई स्थान हैं
जहाँ मैं कभी नहीं पहुँचा
जिनकी कल्पना भी नहीं की
पर यह जानता हूँ
एक अनजान स्थान जाना है।

ऐसा एक क्षेत्र
तुम्हारे नयनों का वह कोना है
जहाँ भविष्य के लिए
संकेत हैं।

तुम स्वयं नहीं जानती
इस रहस्य को -
नयनों पर
जो लिखा है,
उसे तुम नहीं
पढ़ सकती।

16. संवाद

आकाश और पृथ्वी का संवाद
नैतिक प्रश्नों के परे है।

स्वर्ग और नरक का मेल
पुष्प के खिलने के क्षण
में है आधारित।

स्वर्ग एक फुलवारी
जिस में प्रत्येक पुष्प
प्रफुल्लित है
और एक नए फूल
के लिए स्थान।

17. सीमा पार

तब समय की एक अलग
धड़कन थी।

पगडंडी पहाड़ के पार
एक घाटी में आई।

झूमते
विशाल वृक्षों के नीचे
जहाँ खुला स्थान था,
और घूमता झरना था।

अब यह नगर है।
विशाल भवनों के मध्य
पर्यटकों के लिए
एक छोटी धारा है।
पर गगनचुम्बी महालय
हवा में लहराते नहीं।

स्तब्धता है
समय के ताल में अब
एक व्याकुलता।

मन क्षोभ और भय के बीच
खिंच रहा है।

18. मृतक नायक

१

मैं वह नही जो दीखता हूं
मैं स्वयं ही भूत हूं।
जब मैं निर्जीव हुआ
मेरी आत्मा अस्वीकृत हुई
स्वर्ग और नरक को
लडखडाई वापिस तब
मेरे अस्थिपिञ्जर में।

२

हम सुन्दर हैं कि हम मर जाते हैं
जब समय की उडान रुकी
एक क्षण सहस्र वर्ष हुआ
मैं धूल था, एक विचार था
मेरी चाह थी कि शरीर होऊं
क्योंकि मैंने स्पर्श नही किया
भरपूर नहीं
और जब मेरा जमा हुआ शरीर पिघला
प्राणों की सरसराहट से,
वह आनन्द था।

३

शब्द निःस्तब्धता से निकला
स्वतन्त्रता कारागार हो
पर नीरवता

नीरवता को नहीं भाती
हृदय के कांपने को नहीं भाती

पर सौन्दर्य कौन मांगता है
अतः मुझे गीत गाने दो
मुझे घण्टा बजाने दो।

४

मैं हर दिन मृत्यु को
प्रातराश के दूध की तरह पीता हूं
इस प्रभात को जब मैं जागा
श्वेत धूप के धब्बे मेरे कमरे में थे
मैंने रात के वस्त्र पलंग के आस-पास बिखरा दिये
चौकी पर थाल
सुरुचिपूर्ण संजोए थे
कमरे का उपस्कार
ठीक स्थान पर था
वैसे ही जैसे घर जो रुका हुआ है।

मैं प्रातराश खा न पाया।

५

पक्षी उड गये जब में पहुंचा
मैंने दाना हाथों में बटोरा
मेरा पास चाकू न था
पर पक्षी न आये
मेरे हाथ थक गये और गिरते दानों से
पौधे निकले

और श्वेत फूल
कमल भरपूर।

६
मुझे पीने दो
मुझे और पीने दो
जैसे मैं झुका चीत्कार हुआ
नेत्र उठे एक राक्षस देखा
अर्धनर, अर्धनारी
अपने ही वक्ष को पुचकारता हुआ
मैंने देखा कि नदी का पानी
राक्षस की हचकती छाती के साथ
उठ बैठ रहा,
मेरे हाथ का ताल भिन्न है
मैं केवल झाग उठा पाता हूं।

मुझे पीने दो
तो क्या यदि मांस पिघला है
और मेरे हाथों की अस्थियां
पकड नहीं पातीं
जो मैं देखता हूं
अन्धेरा है
चिकित्सा प्रयोगशाला में
मानचित्र जैसा हूं,
पर खोखला तो भरने दो।

७
अन्तिम वेनपक्षी

अग्नि की ओर उडा
जलने के लिये
राख में ढलने के लिये
उठने कि लिये
युवा और निष्पाप।

अग्नि के समीप पहुंचा ही था
आंखें बन्द अन्तिम छलांग सोचता
कि किसी ने कठोरता से खींच लिया --
पुनर्जन्म नहीं था यह --
एक व्यक्ति ने गला दबोचा था
दूसरे हाथ में छुरी थी उसके।

झट दो प्रहार से
उसने पंख काट दिये।

अन्तिम वेनपक्षी
अभी वहीं पडा है
अचल, भावशून्य
निर्जीव
पर मृत भी नहीं
प्राण आंखों में हैं
जो धीरे हिल रही हैं
आकाश की परीक्षा कर रही हैं

निकट आग
कब की बुझ गई।

८

मैं पूरी रात सोता हूं
पर आराम नहीं
पूरे दिन मेरा मन
उदासीन है
और मेरा शरीर
अपरिचित चाह से
अन्धेरे का आकांक्षी है।

कल रात मैंने ठानी
रहस्य को जानने की
घडी का घण्टी लगाई
दो बजे की
जब मैं उठा उस पहर
मैंने देखे पिशाच
मंडराते हुए
रक्त पी रहे।

मेरे हाथ अशक्त थे
सिर में अन्दर
खटखटाहट थी
मैं मूर्च्छित हुआ।

आज मैं उनींदा हूं
अंग पीडित हैं
चाह से
कि अन्धेरा उतर आए।

९ कीडे
मैं जंगले पे खडा
अस्थियों को शरद् धूप में गरमा रहा
मेरी पलकों पर सूर्य किरणें
लाखों बारीक गोलों में बिखरीं
और फिर चींटियां चारों ओर रेंगने लगीं।

वह बहती आईं
मृत्यु की गन्ध जैसी
और कामनाओं को खा गईं।

जैसे मैं कार्यालय में बैठा प्रतीक्षित
वेश्या समान, याद कर रहा,
कितने श्मशान घाट मैंने देखे हैं,
कि वह आईं।

उसके आग्रह पर
अपनी समझ के विपरीत
मैंने उसे बाहों में समेटा।

जब होंठ होंठ से मिले
वह पृथिवी पर ढेर हुई --
मेरी सांस ने
जान ले ली --
मैं पुनः प्रेम नहीं करूंगा।

19. हिमालय प्रयाण

याद हैं वह अंगारे
आग बुझने से बचती हुई
वात उछलती हुई जैसे उपेक्षित भूत
तम्बू के हाथी कान थपथपाते हुए
भूले मानचित्र
जल का सरल नाद
तुम और मैं
हमारी घनिष्ठता?

क्या आवारा बेचारा चले
चीड पेड़ों के बीच से
हमारे पुराने भाई मूर्तिमान
बहुत प्रतीक्षा की इन नें
उनकी याद सो रही है
जब वह जागेंगे
हम सो रहे होंगे,
याद करो।

सुबह जागी है आलसी
अंगों में सुलगती आग
चिड़ियों का आलाप
घास ओस से नील हुई
पलकें फडफडाईं और मुस्कान
ठंडी हवा बीच उडती आई
चलो टीन गर्माएं
और फिर बाल संवारें।

क्या पर्वत बात करता है?
घुमाऊ पथ पर
खुले स्थान पर
पृथिवी की सूजन दीखती है
टूटी शिला के दान्त
यहां और वहां
और निचली ढाल की घास और चरीले से दूर
पर्वत का ध्यानमग्न मुखमण्डल
आंखें बन्द
उदात्त मस्तक, सीधी नाक
और वर्षा के बीच सुन पडता है
इसके वक्ष का धीमा शब्द।

क्या तुमने शरीर दिखाया है
पर्वत नदी को
इसके फेन को चूमा
इससे पीठ को रगडा
और मित्र के साथ मुक्त पाया
इस विशाल स्नानशाला में?
कितनी रुक-रुक के
गर्मी वापस आए
और जब यह फैले
और हम फिर केवल नाम हैं,
समय लौट आया
पर्वत की पट्टी को चढने का।
मेघ के उतरने के बाद

वर्षा का कडक से गिरना

टट्टू काम्प रहे

उनकी उदास विशाल आंखें अन्दर देख रहीं

और एक भूरा चूहा रास्ता सूंघ रहा

अपने जल-भरे बिल की ओर

क्या यह बन्धु पायेगा

या इसे उन्हें ढूंढने

नदी तट जाना होगा?

ऋतु में जादू हैः

जडें पकडे खींच रहीं मिट्टी

जुड गईं चीडशंकु, अविलीद और बिच्छुओं के साथ

ढाल पर फिसलती हुईं।

क्यों जल जोडता है और गिराता है

शक्ति देता है आत्महत्या के पथ पर,

क्यों वात सुखाती है और जमाती,

सूर्य गरमाता है और जलाता,

पृथिवी सहारती है और दबाती,

क्यों तत्त्वसंकर बढता जाता है?

तथापि नये रूप आते हुए चिल्ला रहे

इस पंकिल रक्ती वसन्त में --

उनके शोकगीत कौन गायेगा

उनके घर हिमक्षेत्र में खोदेगा

जंगल के मैदान में आग बनाएगा?

पहाडी पर प्रकाश बिन्दु तारा नहीं

चरवाहा और पत्नी बात कर रहे है

यादें बांटते हुए
दोनों सौ दिन की गन्ध ओढे हुए हैं
माखन, स्वेद, मूत्र, अन्य रस
धरती का आर्द्र
कढी, ओषधी और धुआं
क्यों वह मिटा लें, जो था?
और शिविर मृदु श्वास ले रहा
क्या तुम अन्धेरे का रिरियाना सुन रहे हो
और बालों का त्वचा में अंकुरण?

जैसे रात्रि मीठे से अपनी चादर बना रही
न ऋक्ष और नाहीं भयावक शब्द
शरीर शान्त धरती पर लेटा हुआ,
क्यों मन तब आग्रही मांगता है नई यात्रा
उन पथ पर जहां हम पहले चले थे?
आग और वात
आप और मिट्टी
बहुत हैं हिमालय पर
परन्तु मन दौडता है प्राचीन छायाओं साथ,
विद्यालय और पिता
मित्र और माता
गाडी और वस्त्र,
और पहुचता है पर्वतीय आश्रम।

यह सचमुच व्यर्थ है,
हम आप हैं
हम आप हैं।

20. धागे

जब अनुभूति तर्क में बन्धे
निर्भाव की पीडा
डुबोती है
निर्भाव उपहासते हैं
अवयव जलते हैं
कोशिकाएं पिघलती हैं
अम्ल में।

हा क्या जलना था
अपनी ही आग में?

प्रश्न का उत्तर
दूसरे प्रश्न में है।

वही स्वप्न आये हैं,
दस वर्ष
वही बिम्ब बैठे,
वही भय दबाये,
निर्वाण कैसे हो?

योगिनी छज्जे पर बैठी
पथिकों को कहती सी
मैं अकेली हूं
दूरबोध से।
क्या मैंने सही सुना

चाय के अवशेष परखूं
चित्र दर्पण मे देखूं
छाया मापूं
लाख का मन्त्र पाठ
रोम पर करूं?
हां वह कामुक है
पर शीघ्र ऊब जायेगी।

एक निःशब्द चीख झंझोटती है
गांव के सूअर का प्रेत
धुंध में घुलता सा दीखता है।
दौडता हूं कसाईक्षेत्र
और सूअर वहां है लकडी समान
पांव बंधे, मुंह दबा
उसकी चीखें आकाश फाडती,
चार लंगोटित लोग बहरे हैं
छुरी पैना रहे यह
घर के लिये मांस चाहते।

उस शाम को व्रत है
पर सूअर की आत्मा के बजाय
मेरे विचार भटकते हैं
और रुकते हैं आनन्द की पुत्री पर
मेरे मन्दिर पर षोडशी उपासिका
वह स्पर्श से स्फटिकमय है,
अतः मैं उसे रहस्य बतलाता हूं
अस्तित्व और शून्यता का।

मेरी चाह इतनी है
कि चाह ही इसकी पूर्ति है।

119

मेरी चाह इतनी है
कि चाह ही इसकी पूर्ति है।

21. एक ताल, एक दर्पण

१

जैसे फूल की गिरती पंखडी
शाखा को लौटे
ऐसी थी तितली की उडान।

२

शरद की झंझानिल में
व्याघ्र और हरिण
साथ ठिठुरे।

३

मध्याह्न की गर्मी में
जल से भाप उठी,
पुराना संगीत
कान में गूंजा --
ताल ही दर्पण है।

४

झांझा अति पीडित
तितली नहीं बनेगा।

५

फुलवारी के शृंगार
और पक्षियों के कोलाहल के मध्य
देखो पीपल का धैर्य।

६

लगता है तरबूज़ को नहीं मालूम
रात तूफान आया।

७

चांद को देखते देखते
मेरी गर्दन दुखाई।

८

वसन्त का पहला गीत गाते
पक्षी शर्मीला लगता है।

९

कितने तीर्थ जाकर
आकाश गंगा
उतनी ही दूर।

१०

यात्रयों के साथ
पक्षी भी डेरा डाले।

११

पुरुष बैठे करे ध्यान--
कठोर परिश्रम।

१२

डाकू साधूवेश में हैं
कवि ने
तलवार बान्धी है।

१३

मैं हंस से खेलने चला
पर उसकी उडान से
डर गया।

१४

चिडियाघर के पिंजरे
का भालू
मुझे भाई लगा।

१५

दर्पण में बिम्ब
धुंधलाता है।

१६

इस रात देर
मेरा साथ कौन जगा है?

१७

मैना ऐसे गाये
जैसे पिंजरे में है ही नहीं।

१८

विशैले छत्रक
सुन्दर लगते हैं।

१९

पक्षी की कूक सुनकर
जल में चन्द्रमा हिला।

२०

चन्द्रमा दौड रहा
एक मेघ से दूसरी ओर।

२१

अरुषी ने ओस के बिन्दु को
अंगुली में पकडना चाहा।

२२

सुन्दर है
पतझड की शाम का चन्द्र
जीवन की शाम में।

२३

तितलियां इधर उधर भाग रहीं
बीते वसन्त को ढूंढतीं।

२४

पाला और भीषण पडा
अब पुष्प नहीं खिलेंगे।

२५

काश गिरती बर्फ पर
तितलियां मंडरातीं
कैसा गातीं वह।

२६

चोर ने हार चुराया

पर चन्द्रमा मेरी खिडकी के बाहर
से नहीं भागा।

२७

मछलियां
गिरते फूलों के डर से
चट्टान नीचे छिप गईं।

२८

श्मशान में
बहुतेरी सुन्दरियों की अस्थियां हैं।

२९

गर्मी की रात
पिंजरे का कोई पक्षी
नहीं सोया।

३०

सुन्दर है
शरद चन्द्रमा
पर हमारी खिडकियां बन्द हैं।

३१

अरुषी बहुत रोई
पूर्ण चन्द्रमा के लिये।

३२

तूफान के झोंके पर बैठी

मन्दिर की घण्टी की आवाज़
चली आई।

३३

बिन जाने कैसे समझूं
ग्रन्थ मैं लौटाता हूं।

३४

पतंग पर किरणें हैं
जब ताल पर अंधेरा आ चुका।

३५

तूफान में कुत्ते
गिरते पत्तों पर भौंक रहे।

३६

प्रकाश
बिम्ब बिम्ब का प्रतिरूप
रूप रूप का प्रतिबिम्ब।

३७

सुन्दरता क्या निहारूं
वसन्त के पग
निरन्तर दूर हो रहे।

३८

कौवे शोर मचा रहे
कि कोकिला को सुन न पाएं।

३९

मां कि गोद में सुरक्षित
भिखारी बच्चे को क्या मालूम
ठंड कितनी है।

४०

चिडिया घोंसला बनाए
पेड पर, कैसे बताएं
पेड कटने वाला है।

४१

उदास लगे पिंजरे का पक्षी
जब तितली देखे।

४२

जुगनू रोशनी दें
बच्चों को
जो उन्हें पकडें।

४३

नाग जल निर्मल है
पांव कैसे धोऊं।

४४

अनजान कि वसन्त जा रहा
तितली घास पर सोई।

४५

वह पास से निकला

पर सवेरे के कुहरे में
उसे पहचान न सका।

४६
हरिण स्तम्भित हुआ
उछलते बाघ की
भीषण सुन्दरता देख।

४७
आतिशबाज़ी बाद
दर्शक लौटे
अब वीराना है।

४८
मकडे जाल से
तितलियों के पंख
लटक रहे।

४९
उपवन में प्रत्येक पेड
का अपना नाम है।

५०
पतङ्ग धरती गिरा
निरीक्षण से जाना
आत्मा नहीं।

५१
मधुमक्खी बार बार

देवता की मूर्ति पर
वार कर रही।

५२

कितने मूर्ख हैं जो
इशारों का दाम करते हैं।

५३

गंगा की लहरों पर
चांद चित्र बना रहा।

५४

पक्षी हंस रहे
कि हमारे पास समय नहीं।

५५

चांदनी में सब वस्त्र
सुन्दर लगते हैं।

५६

खण्डहर में मैंने
कई फूल उगते पाए।

५७

रुई का फेरीवाला
गर्मी से पीडित।

५८

मेंढक पत्ते बैठ
कुल्या को पार किया।

५९

यदि पपीहा पौधा होता
लोग गीत काट लेते
रेशमी रुमालों
और पन्नों बीच
सुखाने के लिए।

६०

आज भी
सूर्यास्त हुआ
फुलवारी में
बेचारे तारे
शरद के चांद से
हारे।

६१

तूफान के शोर में भी
चिडिया की पुकार आई।

६२

सर्दी की फुहार
मुझे मिलने से पहले
फुलवारी हो आई।

६३

भुर्जतरु भीषण वर्षा में
सोए पडे।

६४

पपीहा कूक करे
पर कोई न आया।

६५

शाम हो चली
मेरी बेटी
चुपचाप रसोई में
खाना खा रही।

६६

कमल सुन्दर है
पर नाविक बहरा।

६७

कारागार के आंगन में भी
पुष्प खिले।

६८

मैं थक गया
क्या नींद में भी
पुष्प खिलेंगे।

६९

पूजा करते
पुष्प मुरझाए।

७०

कोमल फूलों पर
वर्षा मूसल सी गिर रही।

७१

शरद की चांदनी में
मेरा बालक
गोद नहीं।

७२

पड़ोसी की उंची दीवार
न वह देखे नदी
न दूर पहाड़ी।

७३

रात अंधेरे के तम्बू में
छिप गया ताल
पर हंस का स्वर
कोमल और श्वेत है।

22. मन्दिर की सीढियां

१

मेरे समछाया के आंगन में
पपीहे ने पहला गान किया।

२

मालूम नहीं कहां से यह गीत
धरती पर गिर आया।

३

मचान से देखते
बाघ कितना सुन्दर लगता है।

४

तितली मेरे हाथों में
देखते देखते मर गयी।

५

देखो! पर्वत
कम्बल के नीचे सोया है।

६

पुष्प खिले
दूसरे दिन
हिमपात हुआ।

७

मैं फूलों को
चुनना नही चाहता
पर घर कैसे लौटूं
चुने बिना।

८

पता नहीं किन फूलों की
सुरभि फैल गई
आंगन में।

९

बादल कभी कभी
चान्द को ढक लेते हैं
ताकि हमारी निहारती आंखें
थक न जाएं।

१०

देखो इस पत्ते से गिरका
जलबिन्दु
कैसे विभाजित हुआ।

११

पपीहे की चीख सुनकर
मुझे स्वर्गवासी दादा की
याद आई।

१२

चान्द की कितनी
समदृष्टि है।

१३

नववर्ष के उत्सव के लिये
मेरे पास नव वस्त्र कहां?

१४

ओठ ठिठुरते हैं
इन हवाओं में।

23. डरा पक्षी

कांपते, रात के तूफान में
बिजली की चौंध में
नष्ट नीड देख कर
वह लौटा घर निराश।

विश्व सिकुड गया था तब
कोई दूसरा नहीं
जो अपने जैसा रहा।
नहीं ढूंढना अब कोई।

भूमि बहुत अलग सी थी
रेत थी मकान थे
ध्रुव ऋतु समान सी
न धूप थी न चांदनी।

खिडकी में जब देखता
बन्धु उछल रहे
पंख भरते उडान
यह दृश्य गोच कर।

नल की फुहार बनी
उस की बरसात अब
सुदूर भूले देश में
रिमझिम पानी गिर रहा।

24. मिट्टी का अनुराग

देश प्रेम कहां से उभरता है?
हमारे कूचे कीचड वाले थे
और भय था
बाजार के गुंडे
पीट न लें।
चुप रहना सीखा
अज्ञात भीड में
पिघल जाना।

यह सच है --
पतझड की हवाएं
तीखी और सुहावनी थीं
और नदी के पास
उपवन में भागना
पहाडी से लुढकना
आनन्दमयी था।

पुरखों की कहानियां
रोमांचित थीं
उनसे जुडी हुई
मैंने भी कई कथानक बुने।

पर अन्य देशों की भी
अपनी कहानियां हैं
सुन्दर घाटियां

पर्वतीय नदियां
सुन्दरियां।

अन्तर शायद है
बचपन में
मैंने देश की
मिट्टी खाई।

यह देश मोह नहीं
मिट्टी का अनुराग है।

25. विस्मृति

क्योंकि विस्मृत हैं हम,
नया जन्म नहीं
हो सकता हमारा।
बंधे हैं हम
अतीत में,
अन्धे समान।

चिह्नप्राप्ति
जीवन का लक्ष्य
एकमात्र --
भक्ति,
याचना,
योग।
आतुरता,
पूर्ण होकर पीडा की,
मधु को चखकर
विष पीने की।

काल की
सृजन भी देखी है
हमने अभी,
अतीत भविष्य को
गर्भ समेटे,
प्रस्फुटित
हुआ नहीं।

इसका जन्म
मायावी होगा
इसका शोषण है
स्मृतिधारा
ऊर्जा है
स्वरों की झंकार।

पर यह यायावर मन
इन्द्रजाल की
भूलभुलैया में
भटक गया
विस्मृति की प्रतिगूंज
सुनकर
सम्मोहित।

26. सोता चरागाह

दोपहर की
तपतपाती धूप में,
सोते चरागाह में,
जन्तु
पेड की छाया में
फैले हुए थे,
मधुमक्खियां ही
तल्लीन थीं
फूलों के ऊपर।

सामान्यता का रेशमी आवरण
ढके था
इन्द्रियों को
भ्रमों से।

उस तपन में
चाह उठी
निशब्दता की
पत्थरों की
बिन कहानी
जो बतायेंगे
धरा में
कितनी गर्मी है।

उस फटे आकाश में
न मृत्यु थी
न पानी
घर से पहुंचकर
दूर
एक आलोक में थे
जहां से वापस निकलकर
आना मना है।

27. प्रहेलिकाएँ

मैं, जो यह गीत गा रहा हूँ,
कल अपने शब्द भी पहचान न पाऊँगा
इस स्वर का जादू मिट गया होगा

निस्तब्ध अपने को टटोलते हुए
बिन भूत, भविष्य या कबः
यह योगी कहते हैं।

मेरा अपना विश्वास है
कि मैं स्वर्ग या नरक का अधिकारी नहीं।

भविष्यवाणी न होः हर एक की कहानी
घुल जाती है अंगराग की भांति।

फलक पर केवल एक अक्षर है
और कुछ निमेष बंधे हुए
जिनसे अतीत की कसक होती है।

वैभव और प्रताप की अन्धी कौंध के आगे
मृत्यु का अनुभव कैसे होगा?

क्या स्फोटित विस्मृति पी पाऊँगा मैं
ताकि अनन्तकाल तक रहूँ;
पर कभी न रहा हूं।

28. आज और कल के बीच

हर छाया में मैं शकुन ढूँढता हूं।

समय का क्रम ऐसा था,
जैसे बाघ की तीव्र छलांग
या मृग की उन्मत्त दौड,
और अब इसके पंख
तितली की तरह थरथराते हैं।

मैं पल के आवरण में ही खो गया।
फिर भी मैंने नीले आकाश को देखा
और एक, उंचे नग्न पर्वत को
जिसके आगे गहरी दरार थी,
और दूसरी ओर हरित पथ
पीपल की कतारों से आंचलित
वक्रा नदी की ओर जाता हुआ।

इस पथ पर मैं दोनों दिशाओं
की ओर चला हूं।

यह पल मुझे दूर ले जाता हैः
मेरे पिता मेरी अवस्था के हैं।
अपने बालपन से मैं
अपने बच्चों को देखता हूं।

रास्ते ऊभरते हैं
और फिर मिट जाते हैं,

प्रतिछाया में ही हम सिमट जाते हैं,
भूख और तृष्णा से पीडित
हम छटपटातें हैं।

अपरिमित को एक में पाया
और एक को खण्डित देखा।

भयभीत,
मैंने धरती को कदमों से मापा।
विचित्रता कुछ दूर हुई।

29. मृत्युशय्या

मृत्यु एक रहस्य है
जिसे मैं व्यर्थ नाम से बांधता हूं।

जीवन एक बांध है
और मृत्युशय्या पर बांध की दरारें
दीखती हैं,
बीते दिनों का आभास,
कुछ क्षण।

एक आशा उठती है
कदाचित स्मृति का सीमेंट
बांध की दरारों को जोड लेगा।

पुष्पों से छिपे शव को देखकर
विचार उठता है
हर क्षण
रंगे कागद पर नल की बूंदों की तरह
भीतर चित्र मिटाता है।

शब्द व्यर्थ हैं
जब हम रो सकते हैं,
पर मां की गोद का
चैन कहां।

केवल बीते दिन की सुगन्ध
बची है।